POOR FOLK'S PLEASURE

I0140049

Len Jenkin

BROADWAY PLAY PUBLISHING INC
224 E 62nd St, NY, NY 10065
www.broadwayplaypub.com
info@broadwayplaypub.com

POOR FOLK'S PLEASURE
© Copyright 2005 by Len Jenkin

First printing: December 2005
I S B N: 0-88145-299-8

Book design: Marie Donovan
Word processing: Microsoft Word
Typographic controls: Ventura Publisher
Typeface: Palatino
Printed and bound in the U S A

For those extraordinary actors, all of whom have bravely worked with me a number of times, and who lit this one up in the barn from the very beginning: Steve Coats, Saun Ellis, Laura Innes, Will Patton, and Rocco Sisto.

POOR FOLK'S PLEASURE was first presented by
River Arts Repertory Company, Woodstock, New York,
on 15 July 1989, with the following cast and creative
contributors:

Steve Coats
Saun Ellis
Laura Innes
Will Patton
Rocco Sisto

Director .... Len Jenkin
Stage manager ....Rose Bonczek

SCENES

1. Rowing in to Shore, with "I Have a Dog, His Name is....Bill"
2. The Lantern and the Bell
3. Dragging Dance-devil and angel
4. Hi-Hat Tavern
5. Phone Talk with Hitting 1
6. The Man with a City in a Box
7. On the Corner, with "Ants in my Pants"
8. How We Eat in the U S A, with White Courtesy Telephone
9. Fascination
10. Leroy Smiles, the Crab Boy
11. Clown Show 1
12. Frankie the Finn
13. "I have a Boyfriend Fatty"
14. A Woman on the Phone, with "Ants in my Pants"
15. Blind Man and the Lead Girl
16. A Film Extra Talks to the Audience
17. The Man on Crutches, and his Girlfriend
18. Fascination 2
19. Clown Show 2
20. The Man with Shaking Hands, with Hitting 2
21. Do The Stroll
22. In the Tattoo Parlor
23. Dance Call
24. Montage: Frankie the Finn, Fascination Girl on phone, Dragging Dance, Clown Show, Man with Shaking Hands, Boatman-Mandolinist, White Courtesy

NOTE

POOR FOLK'S PLEASURE is a theater piece for five to seven performers. The set should be extremely simple: the bare interior of the theatre, and only those few objects necessary to the understanding of the scenes. Despite the fact that the performers take on a variety of roles, POOR FOLK'S PLEASURE should also feel like a concert for the company as band: a series of interconnected numbers, all coming from the same author and the same ensemble.

Where speech is indicated and no set text is given, this language is to be created by the performers and director, along with dances, staging, and soundtrack.

SONGS

All songs not listed are original or traditional.

In Scene 7: *Ants in My Pants,* Bo Carter
In Scene 21: *The Stroll,* The Diamonds
In Scene 26: *Bring It On Home,* Sam Cooke
In Scene 28: *Life Is But a Dream,* The Harptones

The seperate permission of each copyright holder is required for usage in any live stage production. If that permission is unavailable or unaffordable, please substitute other songs.

1.

(*A* BOATMAN *rows, a mandolin in his lap, and a beatific smile on his face. He spots the crowd on shore, and stops rowing, letting himself drift to a stop. He stands, steps toward the audience, tunes his mandolin. He sings.*)

BOATMAN: I have a dog
His name is...Bill...
He...

(*The* BOATMAN *pauses uncertainly. He exits.*)

2.

(*In the foreground, a lantern and a bell on a small table. Quiet. A* MAN *enters, holding a newspaper. He seats himself behind the table, and reads. He chuckles to himself. Then he folds his newspaper as, one by one, various people approach him, drop a fee into a tin cup on his table, and move to the far end of the space, looking intently at something we cannot see. A hush*)

(*The* MAN *at the table speaks to us, in a language we cannot understand, explaining what the visitors are looking at, his own feelings about it, and the nature of his position there. He falls silent.*)

(*He looks at his watch. He reaches for the bell, and as he does so, we can see his hand shake, so that an effort of will is required for him to raise the bell off the table. He rings the bell, and sets it down. The viewers, one by one, exit, again passing by his table. Silence. In the distance one woman, still looking, remains.*)

3.

*(The Dragging Dance. Rock music: uptempo and strong.
A silent and dreaming ANGEL, borne on the back of a wildly
gesticulating and prancing DEMON, comes toward us.
They pause a moment, and then the DEMON begins to
back away, carrying the still dreaming ANGEL with him.
The music ends abruptly.)*

4.

(A SALESMAN, seated in a chair)

SALESMAN: I believe I'm in a hotel. I'm sure of it. I've
been in them before. Not exactly like this one. Similar.
I have no concept of why my employers imagined I
would be able to sell here. The planet's dead. I think
I'll watch some local television. Uh oh. No television
in my room. I'll go down to the T V viewing lounge,
in the hotel basement.

(He moves to another area, where a MAN watches television.)

SALESMAN: The T V is already on. Kirk Douglas in
Spartacus. A man is watching....
I think it's the same man who welcomed me at the
desk......hmmm....

*(A portion of Spartacus is performed, live: noble Romans
with British accents, Kirk, slaves, etc. The MAN watching
turns off the T V.)*

SALESMAN: Now he's not looking at the T V anymore,
but at a picture that hangs on the wall nearby. It's of a
young girl. *(To MAN)* Excuse me. I'd like to pester you
with some salestalk, if I may.

MAN: Look at her. Carefully. Tell me what you see.

SALESMAN: She looks very pretty...and a little sad. Perhaps she lost her...

MAN: She was a murderess. Sally was removed— ten years ago—for the murder of my brother Arnold in this very room of this hotel. She murdered him with that fire-ax hanging over there on the wall. It was a summer day. The guests were in the T V lounge, viewing. It was just after lunch. My brother was sitting in *that* chair, counting his loose change. Sally came across the room, the fire-ax cradled in her arms, humming a hymn... *(Sings)* Row...row...row... row your boat, gently down the...stream...

SALESMAN: Perhaps I'd better....

MAN: She was my wife. She never knew that... Why don't you take a walk in the reality? Go on. You'll feel better. Go down to the Hi-Hat Tavern. Watch the show.

(The MAN *returns to* Spartacus, *which returns, live— and then he and his T V are gone.)*

(The SALESMAN *walk. Around him, streetscenes of violence, horror. A strange looking* WOMAN *hisses at him from a corner.)*

SALESMAN: I believe that I'm on the kind of street where they cut your throat to get your hat. Interesting, but I better be careful. I believe I'm lost. Ah—there's the Hi-Hat Tavern down that way, with that glowing hat and that glass with bubbles....

WOMAN: You don't want the Hi-Hat Tavern. They all just lie there. Now I can get into almost anything.

SALESMAN: I'd like to pester you with some salestalk, if I may.

WOMAN: You know, you're dead meat, darling. But that's all any of us are anyway. Just meat.

SALESMAN: Is that true?

WOMAN: Just as true as anything else.

(The Hi-Hat Tavern appears. The WOMAN *notices...)*

WOMAN: Excuse me.

(The WOMAN *is gone. In the Hi-Hat Tavern, the* SALESMAN, *an* M C, *and a* GIRL *with her head lying on a table.)*

M C: *(Solemnly)* SHOWTIME!

SALESMAN: Can you help me? I'm lost.

(The M C *raises up the* GIRL'*s head, shows her the* SALESMAN, *and steps aside. Though she becomes more alert as he goes on, and looks at the* SALESMAN *curiously, the* GIRL *doesn't reply to his "conversation".)*

SALESMAN: Can you show me the way back to my hotel?
Is there anything wrong?
Can I get you a drink?
I have traveler's checks.
Are you free this evening?
I know a good discotheque.
Shall we go to the cinema?
I'll pick you up at your hotel.
Can I see you again tomorrow?
Where do you come from? I'm here on a business trip.
The planet's dead. What business are you in?

GIRL: I'm dancing at the Hi-Hat Tavern. That's where we are now.

SALESMAN: Is this your favorite kind of work?

GIRL: I've done it all. Right here. Mud wrestling, executive secretary, bikini boxing, Empress of China. You name it, I've done it.

SALESMAN: What kind of career plans do you have?

GIRL: Just dancing.

SALESMAN: Are you happy now?

GIRL: What are you talking about?

SALESMAN: I'm sorry. I don't understand. Could you say all that again, more slowly. Repeat yourself.

GIRL: Forget it, Mister. Forget all about it. Go home.

(The M C grabs the girl from behind.)

M C: *(Softly)* Showtime!

GIRL: Hey...I gotta go on.

(The M C lays her head back down on the table, as it was before. She appears to sleep. He stands alongside her. Silence. The SALESMAN looks at them, then steps toward the audience.)

SALESMAN: Excuse me. I'd like to pester you with some salestalk, if I may.

5.

(A TEENAGE GIRL talks on the telephone to a friend of hers: boys, clothes, problems. At the same time, the rest of the performers, in pairs, in a kind of Hitting Dance, slapping each other repeatedly across the face, hard and realistically, in a steady rhythm. One of them, interrupts the TEENAGE GIRL on the phone, drags her over to join him. The TEENAGE GIRL is hit, and hits back, repeatedly. At first she laughs, then breaks into sobs and tears. The hitting continues.)

6.

(A MAN holding a shoebox moves rapidly and suspiciously from place to place. The OTHER MAN notices him.)

OTHER MAN: What you got in there?

MAN: Gimme a dime.

OTHER MAN: What for?

MAN: You wanna look, don't you?

OTHER MAN: I just asked what you got in there.

MAN: Fuckin' freeloaders. You understand English?
You gimme ten cents American, I let you look.

OTHER MAN: It don't bite or nothing?

MAN: It don't bite. Make up your mind. I ain't got all
day. I got things to do. Things.

(The OTHER MAN *hands the* MAN *a dime. The* MAN
carefully removes the lid of the box. The OTHER MAN
peers inside.)

OTHER MAN: It's dark in there.

MAN: Yeah. It's night time.

OTHER MAN: What?

MAN: Just look a little closer.

OTHER MAN: It looks deep. You got some kind of trick
box here?

MAN: Yeah, sure. It's a trick box.

OTHER MAN: There's some lights...hey, it's like looking
down on someplace from an airplane. Look at all those
little lights. Hey, man, you make this?

MAN: I didn't make it. I found it.

OTHER MAN: *(Reaching into the box)* Hey, they're
streetlights! It's like a toy...

MAN: Keep your hands outta there. You don't get
to touch for no dime. Just look.

OTHER MAN: Hey...now I can see cars moving...
and stores...Christ. There's little people walking
around in there. This a movie or something?

MAN: Yeah. It's a movie or something.

OTHER MAN: Look it that. A girl is standing on this little streetcorner, realer than hell. You ever see this?

MAN: What's she wearing?

OTHER MAN: A kind of short red dress...

MAN: She going into an apartment building The Raleigh towers? In a hurry, like she...

OTHER MAN: No. She's just standing there, staring at the back of her hand. Ah-she's got a tiny smudge of lipstick on a knuckle. She wipes it away. Now this man is coming over...an' he starts talking....

7.

MAN: Why didn't you come over where we're at? I was waiting. You scared or something?

GIRL: We had homework. 'Sides, I don't like Rat.

MAN: The Rat's in the hole. They picked him up last night.

GIRL: He'll be out by s'afternoon.

MAN: Uh uh. Rat's got a hundred dollar bail. For Rat, that's a life sentence.

GIRL: So?

MAN: What you mean, so?

GIRL: Just so.

MAN: So Rat ain't gonna be home. That's what I'm telling you.

GIRL: I don't like Petey either. He makes me nervous, 'cause he's always so fucked up an' all.

MAN: Petey's in the hole too. He was with Rat. So you can come over any time. Be nobody to bother you. Just me an' Toad. You bring any your girlfriends you wanna bring. Toad got his check last week so we hit the supermarket. Got a frig fulla beer, and bought all these chips an' shit cause you an' your friend was coming. You didn't show, but we didn't eat 'em. I saved all that shit for you, little sister.

GIRL: What'd they do?

MAN: Who?

GIRL: Rat. Petey an' Rat.

MAN: They busted a window.

GIRL: Bull shit.

MAN: They got high an' went downtown. That's all. I wasn't there. Two uniforms an' a cop in plainclothes come over to the house last night. Toad was stoked, an' playing that same Captain Beefheart album over and over again, the way he likes..."Dust blows forward, an' the dust blows back...."

GIRL: What'd they want?

MAN: Who can understand what the police want? Not me, little sister. They went through all of Rat an' Petey's shit. Petey got all his shit in this trunk, man, and it was locked, but them fuckers didn't blink. One of the uniforms just goes out an' gets a tire iron an' fuckin' cracks it. Petey is gonna be mad. Those bastards don't give a shit about anyone's rights. They found Petey's stash, but I'm not sure they'll ever figure out what it fuckin' is. He takes weird shit, an' he mixes it with all that stuff the doctors give him for his head.

GIRL: So what'd they do?

MAN: I told you what they did. You coming over tonight?

GIRL: Maybe.

MAN: What's that shit, *maybe*?

GIRL: That is you just wait there, an' eat potato chips, an' see what happens. "Dust blows forward, an' the dust blows back...." I gotta go...

(A MAN IN STRAW HAT appears in the distance. He looks at the couple, then the audience. He sings, with great passion, a slow blues.)

MAN IN STRAW HAT:
It makes no difference, anywhere you go
Cause I got something, want you to know
I got ants, in my pants, baby for you!

Anytime I come, and feel your charms
It makes my feelings, just get all wrong
Cause I got ants, in my pant, baby for you!

8.

(A MAN with a camera. In the distance, a family: FATHER, MOTHER and CHILD. The FATHER reads the paper, the MOTHER knits, and the CHILD watches T V, as if the MAN with the camera was on it.)

MAN: I work for *Thrills* magazine. Hey, how low can you go? And for how long? I'd quit, and do something a little less slimy, but I gotta eat. Don't we all.

FATHER: I like chicken pot pie.

MOTHER: Not me, Charlie.

CHILD: Daddy...shhhh.

MAN: Hey, no time for reflection here. I'm working. The job? To photograph Miss Charlene Mason, in the nude, these photographs to go with the centerfold theme for December. "I'm in love with Santa."

CHILD: You better watch out, you better not cry, you...

MOTHER: Shhh...

MAN: "Make her jump off the page" they told me.
Charlene is actually an ex-hooker named Alberta
Vignones who I hired for fifty bucks. The part of Santa
will be played by yours truly, facing away from the
camera. Cheaper that way. Don't have to hire some
scuzzball with tattoos. Renting the suit was bad
enough...got it right here in the bag, beard and all.
Alberta lives out along 509 with a kid and a husband
named Charlie or something who works at a sand and
gravel pit moving dirt around. He don't like her doing
the posing every now and then, but they need the
money. Wouldn't you? Same old story.
So I'm heading out toward Alberta's and I'm thinking
I could eat something so I pull into this shopping mall.
There's a place in there called the Wagon Wheel and
I'm thinking uh oh I don't got my bowling trophy and
then I figure what the hell and go in past the Pac Man
machine and slide into the tufted leather and a blonde
cowgirl is moving toward me in a little short white skirt
that's got the skull of a cow on it in rhinestones and I
think "Keep calm and don't do anything crazy" and she
says "Welcome to the Wagon Wheel. You know what'd
you'd like?" and I say "O my God" and she says "Scuse
me?" and I say "Tuna melt, order of fries and a coffee."
She says "Right" and I'm watching her go, little skirt
flipping this way and that, and at that very moment
some fools plays the jukebox and they dim the lights
for the evening dating trade and I say to myself "O K.
It's time to play all the cards you got."
I wait. She comes back with the food like I knew she
would and I give her time to set it down before I say
"Honey, what time do you get off?" And she says
"Can't you boys leaving a working girl alone?" "Not
when they're as pretty as you, Miss" I say. She says
"Just shut up and eat or I'll call the manager. I don't
need to get hassled by every slob who walks in the
door." She goes off, leaving me in bitterness and pain,

and I take a bite, and another, and its not bad. And that's how we eat in the U S A. Some of us, anyway.

FATHER: I like chicken pot pie.

MOTHER: I'm making meatloaf, Charlie.

CHILD: Tuna melt, order of fries, and a coffee.

(The MAN *with the camera is gone, but the family remains. Silence)*

AMPLIFIED VOICE: Mister _____*(Last name of actor playing the* FATHER*)*, Mister _____ _____ *(First and last names of actor playing* FATHER*)*. Please pick up the white courtesy telephone.

FATHER: I'm not expecting any call. I know. Must be for somebody else with my name. But I better check it out. *(Goes to phone, picks it up)* Hello?...yes... This is _____ _____... Who is this? ...IS THIS SOME KIND OF A JOKE?

9.

(A bell rings. We see a silent row of "Fascination" players. Behind them, on a raised platform, a TEENAGE GIRL *who runs the game. Fascination is an old-fashioned storefront game, where the players pay to roll rubber balls toward a set of holes, trying for a prize-winning pattern. The* TEENAGE GIRL *rings the bell again. While she speaks, between games, the players are distracted, their attention wandering....)*

TEENAGE GIRL: We have a winner, we have a winner! Number 18. Seven tickets, any prize, bottom row. Known from the rock-bound coast of Maine to the sun-kissed shores of California, it's Fascination. Time for another game of Fascination. Time for another game of Fascination. *(Rings bell)* Roll'em up! Roll 'em up! And the first ball is out.

(The game has begun, and the players, though remaining still and not miming any playing, have become attentive, focused in front of them, tense.)

(Silence...)

TEENAGE GIRL: *(Rings bell)* We have a winner! We have a winner. Number... *(And continuing....)*

(She repeats her spiel, word for word, except that the number of the winner has changed. As she speaks, the players repeat their distraction, and then their focus when the game begins again. Four games of Fascination. During game 3 the TEENAGE GIRL *makes a phone call to her boyfriend, and we hear her talking to him as the game is in progress. She needs to ask him to "Hold on" when a winner comes up, and then she repeats her speech as before, and resumes her conversation as the following game is played.)*

(In the middle of the fourth game, the players break focus, exit. The TEENAGE GIRL, *busy on the phone, at last notices they're all gone. A bit disturbed, she asks her boyfriend to:)*

TEENAGE GIRL: Hold on. I'll be right back. *(And she quickly exits.)*

10.

*(*LEROY SMILES *appears. He is seated on a low stool. He is legless, and has only two large digits on each hand. A* NEWSMAN *appears.)*

NEWSMAN: LEROY SMILES, THE CRAB BOY! YOU BE THE JUDGE! Smiles, legless, and with only two digits on each hand...

*(*ZACK PAYNE *and* SMILES's DAUGHTER *appear)*

NEWSMAN: ...is accused of murdering Zack Payne, thirty-five, and his own fifteen year old daughter. LEROY SMILES, THE CRAB BOY!

(The NEWSMAN *is gone. The three still figures onstage go into action.)*

SMILES: Ungrateful little bitch! I swore I wouldn't go up on the platform again, and I went up there. I went up there in Dayton, and Akron, and I did some-fuck suburb of Cincinnati where they had us on the asphalt. In a shopping plaza, Miss.

DAUGHTER: We went for a ride is all. Zack's got a car. He bought it from working. It's a Chevrolet. Caprice.

SMILES: Why was I on the platform, 'stead of watching T V, and relaxing in my own personal home? You know why, son? Zack? You know why, Zack?

ZACK: No.

SMILES: So's I could pay the investigations place one thousand dollars to send some sonofabitch to find you. He found you, Miss. You went for a ride all right. Cross three states.

DAUGHTER: You didn't need to do that. I was coming back anyway.

ZACK: We're gonna get married.

(A long beat while SMILES *takes in this information.)*

SMILES: Miss, I ever keep you home from school to do for me? One day?

DAUGHTER: No, you always been...

SMILES: Come here, Zack.

ZACK: What for?

SMILES: I want to show you something.

ZACK: Oh yeah? Like what?

SMILES: You ever seen my hands, Zack?

ZACK: Yeah, sure I seen 'em.

(SMILES *lowers himself off his chair, and begins to scuttle across the floor toward* ZACK.)

SMILES: You ever seen them up close?

(SMILES *moves closer to* ZACK, *dragging himself along the floor, and then raises his powerful claws...*)

DAUGHTER: Daddy! Daddy! NO!

(The NEWSMAN *reappears, and as he speaks,* ZACK, SMILES, *and his* DAUGHTER *return to the positions they were in at the beginning of the scene.)*

NEWSMAN: LEROY SMILES, THE CRAB BOY! YOU BE THE JUDGE!

(The NEWSMAN *is gone, and the scene of "Leroy Smiles, the Crab Boy" begins again, recycling.)*

SMILES: Ungrateful little bitch! I swore I...

(...And continuing, until it is interrupted by the scene that follows...)

11.

(One PERFORMER *stands alone, stage center. An* ANNOUNCER *appears.)*

ANNOUNCER: *(Pointing to* PERFORMER*)* The laws of this person's existence are hideously simple. He *(She)* is permitted to suffer, and commanded to amuse.

(The ANNOUNCER *is gone. Music. The "Clown Show." This is simply a desperate attempt by the* PERFORMER *to please the audience, using the barest minimum of words and/or props. He [She] tries one thing after another. At last the* PERFORMER, *anxious and confused, abandons the attempt, to the tune of whatever applause there may or may not be, and walks off. The music stops suddenly. The stage is bare.)*

12.

(In the distance, three WATCHERS. *In the foreground,*
FRANKIE THE FINN. *He holds his head in his hands.*

WATCHER 1: Look!

WATCHER 2: It's Frankie the Finn!

WATCHER 3: Frankie the Finn's in his eighties. In
forty-seven they foreclosed on the twenty acre farm
he'd bought when he and his wife came over from
the old country. She was buried there, in an open field.
They told Frankie the bank owned it now.

FRANKIE: Fuck the bank.

WATCHER 3: Said Frankie the Finn. After he heard he
stood in the middle of the field by his wife's gravestone
and held his big head in his hands for about an hour.
Everyone in town was watching from the road. Then
he walked into his house and set it on fire. He sat there
at the kitchen table with the room burning around him
till the volunteer fire department went in and hauled
him out. He was screaming in Finnish.

*(*FRANKIE *begins to shout and moan in what sounds like a
mixture of Finnish and unintelligible gibberish. He stops
suddenly.)*

WATCHER 3: They shipped him off to the cackle factory.
Ten years later, he gets out, and comes back to town.
He's got disability or something, and he rents a room,
and sits around all day in front of the bank.

*(*FRANKIE *sits)*

WATCHER 3: He speaks only in Finnish now, as if
everyone can understand him, or at least that's what we
thought till a Finnish guy went over to talk to him and
said it wasn't Finnish at all he was speaking. It sounded

a little like it, but it was just nonsense he was saying,
and smiling all the time.
So I guess that's how it is on this bitch of an earth.
For some of us, anyway. How do you like it?

(FRANKIE *begins to speak loudly in his own language,
half Finnish, half gibberish. He walks toward the audience,
gesturing excitedly, shouting. He stops suddenly, then walks
off in silence.*)

WATCHER 1: What'd he say?

WATCHER 2: Fuck the bank.

13.

(*One* GIRL, *alone on stage. She hesitantly begins to sing.*)

GIRL: I have a boyfriend Fatty
He comes from Cincinnati
With forty-eight toes and a pickle on his nose
And this is the way my story...goes.

One day while I was walking
I heard my boyfriend talking
To a pretty girl with a strawberry curl
And this is what he said to her
I L-O-V-E love you
I K; I...
(*She exits.*)

14.

(*A* WOMAN *at a pay phone, on the street.*)

WOMAN: (*On phone*) You want your medicine, you're
gonna have to come down and see a doctor...I tried,
dammit. They wouldn't give it to me...I said everything
you told me. This black bitch of a nurse fills out this

long goddamn form, and then I told her your leg all
swelled up and you couldn't come to the hospital.
"Put her in a cab" she says. I said "Where'm I gonna
get the money for a cab?" She says "Whyn't you take
some of your dope money and put your momma in
a cab?" I hit her with her own goddamn telephone.
Blood was dripping down her nasty face. They called
the security guard, threw me outta there. Everybody in
the 'mergency room was staring. That guard's gonna
remember me. I was screaming. He hadda drag me
through the door... At a goddamn payphone. Look, Ma,
I gotta see somebody, and then I'm coming home...I'll *be*
there. Tomorrow, we'll go down to the hospital. We'll
take a cab. But I ain't going in there. That black bitch'll
have my ass. You gotta go in there by yourself.

(The WOMAN *hangs up the phone. In the distance, the*
MAN WITH A STRAW HAT *appears. He sings, loudly and*
energetically.)

MAN WITH A STRAW HAT: It makes no difference,
anywhere you go
Cause I got something, want you to know
I got ants, in my pants, baby for you!

Anytime I come, and feel your charms
It makes my feelings, just get all wrong
Cause I got ants, in my pants, baby for you!

15.

(A BLIND MAN *appears. He wears dark glasses.*
He moves hesitantly forward, his stick tapping in front
of him. A NARRATOR*)*

NARRATOR: A blind man walks down the railroad
tracks, stick tapping the ties. The track tells him where
to go, but makes him slow, careful. In his pocket, he's
got a Browning automatic. Blind man with a pistol. Old

tracks, no train's run over them for years. Now the ties become rotten, crumbling. The rails twist, run into tall grass, and stop. *(He's gone.)*

BLIND MAN: Little bitch! She's playing with the squirrels. GET OVER HERE! TRACK DIED! Goddamn government doesn't support the goddamn railroads, how's somebody gonna find his way across the goddamn country. Sweeeethearrrt!

(The LEAD GIRL appears.)

LEAD GIRL: I caught one. A little creature to fight you for me. A gnat. Look! He's in the jar. Tonight when you're sleeping I'm gonna slip him up your nostril, and for seven years he'll drill little buzzholes in your brain, and you'll go nuts. The you'll die. The doctors'll crack your skull open and the gnat'll be as big as a pigeon in there, with a mouth of copper and claws of iron.

BLIND MAN: Come closer, so I can hit you.

LEAD GIRL: You've been bad while I've been gone. Beating the bishop. Fly's open. Think so?

BLIND MAN: Shut up and take my hand. To the town. I want a doughnut. With sugar.

LEAD GIRL: No town. Just country. And a sign.

BLIND MAN: Read me.

LEAD GIRL: Ko-ko-mo. Ten miles.

BLIND MAN: Good. Good. I gotta talk to a man in Kokomo, right?

LEAD GIRL: I don't remember.

BLIND MAN: Yes you do. That's why I have the gun.

LEAD GIRL: Someone's coming! A hulking, stumbling woman, with huge breasts. She's blind, like you. She sniffs. She catches your stink on the wind. She's running this way, crazy with love!

BLIND MAN: Bad lie.

LEAD GIRL: Someone's coming. A man this time.

BLIND MAN: I hear him now. Do we need his money.

LEAD GIRL: Shhh, you big bear. Shhh. Be dumb.

(The FOREST RANGER *enters.)*

LEAD GIRL: *(To* RANGER*)* This man's world is as dark as a dog's. Give us a penny.

RANGER: What are you two doing in here? You got a back-country permit?

LEAD GIRL: He's as perplexed as a sheep.

RANGER: You lead him around, right?

LEAD GIRL: Shhh. He'll get violent. Just to pretend he's sensitive to remarks like that. Actually, he doesn't give a shit.

RANGER: What remarks? He's blind, right? That ain't a bad thing to say if it's true.

(The LEAD GIRL *moves close to the* BLIND MAN*.)*

LEAD GIRL: You don't give a shit, do you, you dead hulk. You heaving bag of gristle. You dark tower, you. Ummm...

BLIND MAN: What's he look like? Handsome?

LEAD GIRL: The whites of his eyes are like the blue skin on a hard boiled egg. His nose is like the...

RANGER: Look, you two. The fine's a hundred dollars. I'm trying to give you a break here. Just go back down to the ranger station at Point Lookout and...

BLIND MAN: POINT LOOKOUT?!

LEAD GIRL: *(To* RANGER*)* Now you insulted him.

BLIND MAN: You read Kokomo.

LEAD GIRL: Did I? I don't remember.

BLIND MAN: Little bitch.

LEAD GIRL: He's still here.

BLIND MAN: Is he now? Can he understand anything?

LEAD GIRL: Try him.

BLIND MAN: We are simple travelers, sir, through this dreary orchard of bones. Honest...honest...

LEAD GIRL: Working people.

BLIND MAN: Exactly.

RANGER: All right. I'm calling in a jeep and haul the two of you down to the highway. The fine's a hundred bucks.

BLIND MAN: You see? You see? The flames of hatred and stupidity burn day and night. Kiss him, and make him go away.

(The LEAD GIRL *hesitates, then goes toward the* RANGER, *making a distorted ugly face at him, sticking out her tongue. Then, in a sexy voice...)*

LEAD GIRL: Do you like me?

RANGER: Get away from me, you little slut.

(The LEAD GIRL *goes back over to the* BLIND MAN.*)*

LEAD GIRL: I'm not attractive today.

(The BLIND MAN *grabs the* LEAD GIRL *by the arm, and steps toward the* RANGER.*)*

BLIND MAN: Excuse her, sir. I'm taking her to school now. She's been playing hookey for weeks and weeks. Staying out late at night too, all by herself, looking into ponds in the forest. Listening to the fishes. Haven't you, honey? Don't be ashamed in front of the nice man.

LEAD GIRL: What nice man? He's another country-simple shitface. Shoot him, and let's get going. I'll stay real still. When something moves, it's him.

(The BLIND MAN *draws his pistol. All three of them are motionless. Silence. A* WOMAN *steps into the scene, her back to us, staring at the other three performers. A voice cries:)*

ASSISTANT DIRECTOR: *(O S)* CUT!

16.

(The FILM EXTRA, *with her back to us, remains. The* BLIND MAN, LEAD GIRL *and the* RANGER *walk off to their dressing rooms. The* ASSISTANT DIRECTOR *enters, shouting orders of various kinds to camera people and crew, as he sets up the next scene to be shot: the* BLIND MAN *and the* LEAD GIRL *approach a Donut Shop.)*

(As he does this, the EXTRA *turns to the audience, while she's waiting to perform, and talks. Perhaps the film is* The Fumes of Life, *starring Mia Farrow and Sylvester Stallone. She talks about herself, her part in the film, what she thinks about the story and the stars. The* ASSISTANT DIRECTOR *gives her instructions: to stroll casually towards the Donut Shop. She's nervous. Her "Ready!" call comes then "Action!" She proudly does her simple bit, and the* ASSISTANT DIRECTOR, *perhaps satisfied with the scene and full of praise, perhaps angry and wanting a re-take, calls a break.)*

ASSISTANT DIRECTOR: Ten minutes, everyone! And that *means* ten minutes...

(The EXTRA *glances back at us a moment, and she's gone, along with everyone else.)*

17.

(A MAN ON CRUTCHES *and his* GIRLFRIEND *enter. Street people. The* MAN ON CRUTCHES *is unsteady, mumbling, having taken a few pills too many. One of his legs is clearly hurting. He wobbles forward on crutches, needing her occasional support. His* GIRLFRIEND *is somewhat messed up herself, but she's together enough to keep them going. She does all the talking; comforting him, urging him on, treating him like a bad and stupid child. If she notices the audience it's too ask them for change, or to be annoyed by them.)*

GIRLFRIEND: Why you looking at my boyfriend like that? You got a problem, bitch?

(He stops and, teetering on his crutches, gropes for a pack of Kools in his pocket. He fishes out the crumpled pack, but drops it. The cigarettes fall all over the floor. His girlfriend picks them up, finds an unbroken one for each of them, lights them up.)

GIRLFRIEND: Cigarette party. Now ain't that nice?

(They move off slowly, smoking, her arm around his waist, her talking in his ear, step by step...)

18.

(A bell rings. We see once again the silent row of "Fascination" players. Behind them, on her raised platform, the TEENAGE GIRL *who runs the game. She rings the bell again. While she speaks, between games, the players are distracted, their attention wandering.....*

TEENAGE GIRL: We have a winner, we have a winner! Number 19. Seven tickets, any prize, bottom row. Known from the rock-bound coast of Maine to the

sun-kissed shores of California, it's Fascination. Time
for another game of Fascination. Time for another game
of Fascination. *(Rings bell)* Roll 'em up! Roll 'em up!
And the first ball is out.

*(The game begins, and the players become attentive, focused
in their varying ways. The* TEENAGE GIRL *picks up the
phone and resumes her conversation with a girlfriend while
the players play. She has one eye on the game, and when a
winning number comes up, her girlfriend has to "Hold on".)*

TEENAGE GIRL: *(Rings bell)* We have a winner!
(And continuing...)

*(She repeats her spiel, word for word, except for a new
winning number. A new game begins, and this time,
as she talks again on the phone, she notices something
among the players. She comes down off her platform and
approaches a man at the end of the row.)*

TEENAGE GIRL: Excuse me. If you're not playing the
game you'll have to vacate that seat. We got people
waiting.

*(The man doesn't answer her, but looks confused, and
remains seated.)*

TEENAGE GIRL: Look, we got a policy. No dime, no
hanging around, understand. I don't make the rules.
Look, you...

*(She notices that a winner has hit, rushes back to her
platform, makes her spiel again, interrupting it occasionally
with "Hang on's" to the friend on the phone. Finally a new
game begins, and she can resume her interrupted phone
conversation. But once again she looks down, and sees the
man who's not playing, still in his seat.)*

TEENAGE GIRL: HEY, YOU! MOVE OUT!

*(Suddenly, all the Fascination players get up and exit.
The* TEENAGE GIRL *looks at them going, then grabs the
phone again.)*

TEENAGE GIRL: *(Into phone)* Just hang on a moment.
I'll be right back.... *(She's gone.)*

19.

(One PERFORMER *stands stage center. An* ANNOUNCER
appears, and repeats the introduction given before.)

ANNOUNCER: *(Pointing to* PERFORMER*)* The laws of this
person's existence are hideously simple. He *(She)* is
permitted to suffer, and commanded to amuse.

(The ANNOUNCER *is gone. Music. Another "Clown Show:"
another desperate attempt by a* PERFORMER *to please the
audience, using the barest minimum of words and/or props.
This time the* PERFORMER, *improvising one comic,
frightening or foolish thing after another, manages to
continue until the music ends. He (She)* takes a tentative
and nervous bow, and walks off.)

20.

(A café. At a table, the MAN *we've seen earlier with the
lantern and the bell. He opens a newspaper, reads, laughs to
himself. He has a coffee cup in front of him. Music plays. In
the background, elegant couples dance. The* MAN *reaches for
his cup, and as he does so, his hand begins to shake. The cup
rattles in the saucer. It is only with a great and painful effort
of will that he succeeds in controlling the trembling enough
to bring the cup to his lips and take a sip. Some coffee spills.)*

*(With some shaking still present, he sets the cup down.
He looks about to make sure no one has noticed his weakness.
He regains his air of dignity, and again he reads his paper.)*

(One of the elegant dancing couples stops dancing. They turn to face each other. They begin to slap each other across the face, viciously, loudly, and very realistically. A WOMAN *enters the scene, walks up to the* MAN *with shaking hands, and taps him on the shoulder. He puts down his newspaper, stands, faces her, and they too begin to slap each other, in a strong rhythm, each blow striking home. Someone begins to sob. The hitting continues.)*

21.

(Music. Couples do their particular version of the sixties dance known as **The Stroll,** *sweeping up and back through the space on parallel lines, moving toward and then away from the audience...)*

Come let's stroll, stroll across the floor
Come let's stroll, stroll across the floor
Then turn around, baby, let's stroll some more...
(And the music continuing...)

(At the far end of the path created by the "Strollers," an OLD MAN *sits. He stares out at the doings before him, and occasionally laughs, a heavy, nasty cackle. In front of him, at the floor at his feet, the legless* LEROY SMILES, *the Crab Boy.* SMILES *begins to move forward with the music, between the line of Strollers, propelling himself angrily forward on his hands, his movements punctuated with harsh rasping breaths. He arrives, with great effort, at the point closest to the audience. Here he stops, his breath coming hard, his face twisted with the effort. Up and back, on either side of him, the dancers swirl.)*

22.

(A Tattoo Parlor, and a TATTOOIST *at work on a*
CUSTOMER. *Also, a* MAN *slumped in a chair in a corner,*
a girl, ROOTHIE, *doing her toenails and a* WOMAN
CUSTOMER *who waits her turn, singing to herself.*
Buzz of the needle.)

CUSTOMER: I was one of the best body men in the state
till I fucked up this hand. Look at it. Thing won't even
close...
I been married, once. I give her the goddamn house,
all the furniture. Most of it was damn near new.
I didn't want nothing. Then I figured first time ain't
my mistake, second time would be. What's the use of
buying a cow when you can get the calf? Ninety-nine
percent of goddamn women they all over you. Shack
up with 'em two three at a time. You get tired of 'em,
leave. Shit, if you can't get along, piss on it. Keep gas in
the car, and a hundred dollar bill taped up in the spare.
That's the way I believe in it...
Say I'm just somewhere, waiting for a tree to fall on me,
and she walks on up. Now I got an ass pocket full of
money, and we get a fifth. So next thing you know,
she says "hey, let's go someplace." So we get in the car.
Next thing we think about is where, but we don't think
about it till we're on the highway doing seventy. Well,
you're going, and you figure, after this next drink you'll
figure out something, and by that time the empty flies
out the window...

(The MAN IN CORNER *laughs moronicly.)*

CUSTOMER: Hey, I'm no alcoholic, man. I can take it or
leave it. But I always take it....

(The CUSTOMER *laughs, and the* MAN IN CORNER *laughs*
again. The TATTOOIST *lays down his needle.)*

TATTOOIST: *(To* CUSTOMER*)* Excuse me. *(He approaches the audience.)*

TATTOOIST: You must be eighteen, and sober. Females must be previously tattooed. I don't do firsts on women. It's bad luck.

MAN IN CORNER: Everybody here is fucked up.

(The WOMAN CUSTOMER *approaches the* TATTOOIST, *dwho's resumed tattooing.)*

WOMAN CUSTOMER: Whatcha got?

TATTOOIST: *(To* CUSTOMER*)* Excuse me. *(To* WOMAN CUSTOMER*)* This guy's getting a cross, on fire. And underneath, his name and social security number. So's he won't forget it. Right, Tony?

WOMAN CUSTOMER: That's stupid.

CUSTOMER: *(Tony)* Yeah? You get messed up enough, you forget everything. I don't want that to happen to me again. It's inconvenient.

TATTOOIST: You want that? Your name and number?

WOMAN CUSTOMER: Nah. That's stupid.

TATTOOIST: Look in the book. Roothie, show the kid the book.

*(*ROOTHIE *gets up, and leads the* WOMAN CUSTOMER *to the book of tattoo designs. The* WOMAN CUSTOMER *looks through it.)*

WOMAN CUSTOMER: I want this one. Right over my tit.

ROOTHIE: Can't you read? That one's got a big X through it.

WOMAN CUSTOMER: I don't care. I want it.

ROOTHIE: Sorry. He don't do that one no more.

TATTOOIST: *(To* CUSTOMER*)* You're done. Don't touch it. Let it set a minute and I'll clean you up with some alcohol. *(To* WOMAN CUSTOMER*)* Next.

(The CUSTOMER *leaves the tattooing chair, and takes a seat along one side of the room. The* WOMAN *takes his place, bringing the book with her. She shows it to the* TATTOOIST.*)*

WOMAN CUSTOMER: I want that one.

TATTOOIST: Roothie told you. I don't do that one no more.

MAN IN CORNER: Everybody here is fucked up...

ROOTHIE: *(To* MAN IN CORNER*)* Feed the dogs... FEED THE DOGS!

(The TATTOOIST *begins work on the* WOMAN, *and she begins to tell him a story in a quiet voice as the needle buzzes away. The* MAN IN CORNER *slowly gets up, and crosses the room. As he does so, all fall silent, and become quite still. He exits. For a moment, silence and stillness, and then, as from a great distance, the howling of dogs...)*

23.

(An OLD MAN, *seated, and a* YOUNG WOMAN *standing alongside him. They sing the Dance Call. In another space, a couple slowly turns to the music.)*

OLD MAN & YOUNG WOMAN:
Two little sisters form a ring
Now you're born and now you swing

Clothes all off and your toes are curled
Monkey jumps through that hole in the world

Eat ice cream, drink soda water
Some old man gonna lose his daughter

Drink soda water, eat ice cream
Some young girl gonna lose her dream

Girls and boys walk the same old trail
Same old possum walks the same old rail

Huckleberry shuffle and the clothesline cling
Peppermint twist and the grapevine swing

Round they go and they go around... *(Continuing)*

(The OLD MAN *stands and comes toward the audience, as the* GIRL *continues singing. He's smiling to himself...)*

OLD MAN: *(To audience)* Quit that hugging! ...Ain't you ashamed? ...Heh, heh.... That's better...that's right....

(The OLD MAN *is gone. The couple still turns slowly to the music.)*

GIRL: *(Still singing, more softly)*
Round they go, and they go around
Round they go, and they go around
Round they go, and they go around....

24.

(Music. FRANKIE THE FINN *appears, holding his head in his hands, mumbling to himself. His body jerks and sways, his voice rising and falling in a language we cannot understand.)*

(The TEENAGE GIRL *who runs the Fascination game rushes across the stage, and makes a phone call to her boyfriend: casual, sexy, self-possessed.)*

(One of the performers who previously performed a "clown show" appears, focused on the audience, doing one hopeless, funny or pathetic routine after another.)

(The Dragging Dance, an angelic girl dreaming on the back of a man who writhes and twists like a demon, moves forward and back in the space.)

(The BOATMAN/*Mandolin Player who rowed in to shore at the play's beginning appears, steps toward the audience, tunes his instrument and sings. All the events behind him continue.)*

BOATMAN: I have a dog
His name is...Bill
He.....
(He pauses uncertainly. He exits.)

(The MAN WITH SHAKING HANDS *enters, views the chaotic scene around him with sang-froid, and seats himself at his café table. He opens his newspaper, reads, laughs to himself. He lifts his coffee cup, and his hand trembles violently. The coffee spills.)*

(The TEENAGE GIRL *asks her boyfriend to "Hold on... I'll be right back" and she's gone.)*

(The Dragging Dance is gone.)

(The clown/performer is gone.)

*(*FRANKIE THE FINN *stops mumbling, looks up, and walks rapidly offstage.)*

(The MAN WITH SHAKING HANDS *is alone. Silence)*

AMPLIFIED VOICE: Mister _____ *(Last name of actor playing the* MAN WITH SHAKING HANDS*)*, Mister
_____ _____*(First and last names of the actor playing the* MAN WITH SHAKING HANDS*)*. Please pick up the white courtesy telephone.

MAN WITH SHAKING HANDS: I'm not expecting any call. I know. Must be for somebody else with my name. But I better check it out. *(Goes to phone, picks it up)* Hello? ...Yes... This is _____ _____... Who is this? ...IS THIS SOME KIND OF A JOKE?

25.

(One MAN, *alone onstage. He sings, and dances to illustrate...)*

MAN:
You put your right foot in, you take your right foot out
You put your right foot in, and you shake it all about
You do the hokey-pokey and you turn yourself around
That's what it's all about!

You put your left foot in, you take your left foot out
You put your left foot in, and you shake it all about
You do the hokey-pokey...and you turn yourself
  around....
That's what it's all about!

You put your whole self in, you take your whole self
  out
You put your whole self in...and you shake it all about!
You do the hokey-pokey and you turn yourself around
That's what...

(He pauses uncertainly, and exits.)

26.

(A motel room somewhere. A MAN IN A CHAIR. *A* WOMAN *unpacks groceries from a shopping bag onto a table.)*

WOMAN: Box of Fab, fifty extra strength Tylenol,
Tampax, baby powder, box of these Mister Salty
pretzels, carton of Salem one hundreds, four bananas,
your two beers, Nescafe, creamed spinach, creamed
carrots, and this other jar of mush. That's it....

Hey, it's not like we're gonna be here forever. All this
shit's gonna fit right in the backseat.... Hey, I got this

newspaper at the checkout. Listen to this: this one-legged guy had a pet beaver, and it ate his wooden leg off while he was sleeping. Next morning he went to stand up, an' he just fell over.

(The MAN IN THE CHAIR *remains silent, barely acknowledging her presence, his expression unchanged.)*

WOMAN: Seems like you and me, we're doing life on the installment plan...ten days now and fifteen days there, and ten days later.
Is she asleep in there?

(The MAN IN THE CHAIR *barely nods. The* WOMAN *goes off into the next room. From offstage, we hear her begin to sing quietly.)*

WOMAN: If you ever change your mind
About leaving........

(The WOMAN *emerges, walks slowly toward the* MAN IN THE CHAIR.*)*

WOMAN: *(Singing softly)* ...leaving me behind
Bring it to me, bring all your sweet loving,
Bring it on home to me.

You know I'll always be your slave
Till I'm buried, buried in my grave
Ah, bring it to me...

(The WOMAN *moves next to the* MAN IN THE CHAIR, *and puts her arms around him. He leans his head on her breast.)*

WOMAN: *(Singing softly)*
...bring all your sweet loving,
Bring it on home to me.

27.

(*An* OLDER MAN *comes toward the audience. In the distance, the couple from the previous scene remain.*)

OLDER MAN: When you get up sixty, seventy miles an hour, you figger what the hell am I doing down inside this boxcar? You can't sit down, an' you can't lay down, and you're lucky if you can stand. Always bouncing 'bout three foot off the floor. Ain't a goddamn thing to hang onto. No wonder I got arthritis. It ain't from the war, it's from the fucking boxcars.

One time I'm with Hatcheck Murphy, an' we were going over the hump, only we didn't know we was going that way. Colder'n hell. I had just a T-shirt on, but I had a bottle of hot peppers. I drank the juice off of those peppers, only thing that kept me alive. I was walking the car the whole time, snow blowing in all over the place. Everything outside was white. I said "Lord, where the hell am I at?"

Murphy had him a tokay blanket. He drank the bottle, an' then after awhile, I swear to God, he just lights his cigarette, gets up, and walks out the door. That sonofabitch was doing about sixty mile an hour. I don't know whatever happened to him.

Ain't that something?

28.

(*The* BOATMAN *from the opening scene, rowing once again. With a beatific smile on his face, he pulls away from shore. He rows smoothly. Beside him stands a young girl. She sings, in a very slow rhythm.*)

GIRL: Row, row, row your boat
Gently down the stream

Merrily, merrily, merrily, merrily
Life is but a dream

Row, row, row your boat
Gently down the stream
Merrily, merrily, merrily, merrily
Life is but a dream.

(The entire company joins the BOATMAN *and the* GIRL,
forming a group around them. The BOATMAN *stops rowing.*
All sing, with some doo-wop harmony and back-up.
Beautiful and slow.)

ALL: Life is but a dream, it's what you make it
Always try to give, don't ever take it
Life has its music, life has its songs of love

Life is but a dream, and I dream of you
Strange as it seems, all night I see you
I'm trying to tell you, just what you mean to me

Life is but a dream, and we can live it
We can make a love, none to compare with
Will you take part in, my life, my love—
That is my dream...
Life is but a dream...

(As the song fades away, the MAN WITH SHAKING HANDS
comes forward from the group. In a language we cannot
understand, he begins to explain the song, the performance,
his own life.... He falters, pauses, falls silent. Then, with a
shrug and a smile, he returns to the group. The BOATMAN
begins once again to row, smoothly and steadily. The lights
fade.)

END OF PLAY